Korea's
Natural Wonders

Exploring Korea's Landscapes

KOREA ESSENTIALS No. 9

Korea's Natural Wonders
Exploring Korea's Landscapes

Copyright © 2012 by The Korea Foundation

First Published in 2012 by Seoul Selection
B1 Korean Publishers Association Bldg., 105-2 Sagan-dong,
Jongno-gu, Seoul 110-190, Korea
Phone: (82-2) 734-9567
Fax: (82-2) 734-9562
Email: publisher@seoulselection.com
Website: www.seoulselection.com

ISBN: 978-89-97639-04-5   04080
ISBN: 978-89-91913-70-7   (set)
Printed in the Republic of Korea

Korea's Natural Wonders

Exploring Korea's Landscapes

KOREA
FOUNDATION
한국국제교류재단

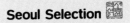

Seoul Selection

Contents

Delving Deeper

INTRODUCTION

For those living in Seoul, it's easy to conclude that the urban swath of concrete grays and muddy browns is all there is to see in Korea. Yet those who look up can glimpse crests of mountains, seemingly faraway yet thankfully ever-present. Such is Korean nature—never imposing or intimidating, forever patiently waiting for us to take notice. In a way, this book was written in the hope of encouraging more readers to take notice of this subdued, yet spectacular, beauty.

Take a look around at the ubiquitous mountains that dot the peninsula (about which more is written in the chapter on mountains). They're hard to miss, as it is said one can see mountains from anywhere in Korea. Or make an afternoon sojourn to any one of Korea's Ramsar-registered inland wetlands. Go for a walk among fields of reeds, or engage in stealthy bird-watching in the hope of sighting endangered species like the hooded crane or Oriental stork. If you still yearn for more exposure to local flora and fauna, consider heading out to one of Korea's seas—of which there are three (being a peninsula, Korea is bordered on three sides by water). The South, East, and West Seas are each distinctive, and the coasts feature foods that are some of the country's most flavorful. If you're in the capital city and ache for a change of pace, go for a walk along the Hangang River, Seoul's most distinctive geographic feature. By bifurcating the city, it created the Gangbuk ("north of the river") and Gangnam ("south of the river") districts, each of which evolved to develop its own personality. The river has witnessed the changes in the city's—and by extension the country's—history, and remains iconic to this day, down to the bridges that crisscross it at 31 points. If you can spare a few days, however, go for an excursion to Jeju-do, Korea's biggest island, and arguably its biggest tourist destination, too. Known for its three "plenties"—wind, rocks, and women—the island is incredibly friendly and welcoming; until recently, the gates there were kept unlocked. Indeed, the popular trekking trails along the coast are named "Olle," meaning, "Won't you come?"

In a sense, this book extends the same welcome to its readers. Won't you come to Korea and experience its natural wonders?

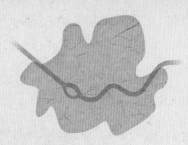

Chapter One

SYMBOL OF SEOUL, THE HANGANG RIVER

Arguably Seoul's most distinctive natural feature, the Hangang River juggles several symbolic roles simultaneously—at once a historical touchstone, a social gathering place, and, of course, a place of natural beauty that is not to be missed.

The fourth longest river on the Korean Peninsula, the Hangang spans a length of approximately 514 km and provides the water that flows into the numerous tributaries that branch out across the city and function as mini-Hangangs unto themselves, offering similar places of refuge for weary urban dwellers. The river itself is sourced by twin Hangangs that emerge from the slopes of Mt. Geumgangsan in North Korea. It bisects the city, a fact that incidentally gave rise to the pseudo-geographical terms "Gangnam" (south of the river) and "Gangbuk" (north of the river) to describe city localities that have each developed their own distinctive character over time. After coursing through the city, the river flows out to the Yellow Sea.

It has evolved over time, first as a witness to many crucial moments in Korea's history, and then as an important landmark next to which prime real estate sprang up. Now, the Hangang River acts as a scenic respite for city residents, a leisure destination for water sports enthusiasts, an outdoor entertainment venue for concerts and festivals, and much more.

BACKGROUND AND GEOGRAPHY

When the Joseon Dynasty (1392–1910) selected Hanyang (modern-day Seoul) as its capital, the Hangang River was no doubt a key consideration. Residents drew their water from the river, which served as a ready conduit for the transport of people and commodities as well. The river was constantly bustling with people and activity, naturally becoming a center of everyday life and commerce from early on. As a community focal point, the river's significance has remained relatively constant, but its surrounding scenery is another story entirely. Vendors lugging bundles on their backs have been replaced by businessmen toting briefcases and

Yeouido Hangang Park

laptops, while the landings that received ferryboats have become massive bridges that accommodate endless flows of traffic.

The name "Hangang" originates from the Korean word *hangaram*. The word *han* is similar to an ancient word that meant "great and sacred." During the Joseon period, sacrificial rituals were performed for the "four great rivers," those that flowed directly into the sea. There was one river in each of the four cardinal directions: the Nakdonggang (east), Daedonggang (west), Yongheunggang (north), and Hangang (south). Foreign documents sometimes referred to the Hangang as the Seoul River.

The Hangang River flows past the village of Misa-ri beneath Paldang Dam, at which point it grows broader and deeper as it passes former landing sites such as Gwangnaru Ferry and Samjeondo. Not far from here is Seoul's Apgujeong district, where Mt. Namsan silently overlooks the river's flowing waters. This mountain is described in the poetry by Lee Byeong-yeon: "As the light of the morning sun dances on the Hangang River / I can dimly see the fishing boats between the mountain peaks." At its foot is the district of Itaewon. Here, the river reaches Noryangjin ("heron crossing ferry"), so named because of the herons that used to frequent the area. Noryangjin was one of the three ferry sites along the Hangang River in Seoul, in addition to Yanghwajin and Hangangjin.

As the river flows downstream, its bed gradually broadens and its waters flow more slowly. Because of the slower flow, the sand and silt carried along by the water from upstream areas are deposited onto the bed, where they accumulate. Over time, this process has created several islands along the river, including Namiseom, Yeouido, and Bamseom, as well as a number of uninhabited islets. Yeouido, formerly a place of exile during the Goryeo Period, is close to the Mapo Ferry (also called Samgae Ferry). Grain from all around the country used to be transported by barge along the West

Jeongseon drew the landscape of Mt. Namsan in response to his friend Lee Byeong-yeon's poetry. (*Mokmyeokjodon*, Jeongseon, 17th c., Gansong Art Museum)

Sea, up the Hangang River, and on to Mapo Ferry and Yongsan Ferry, where they were stored in warehouses such as Gwangheungchang and Daeheungchang.

HISTORY OF THE HANGANG RIVER

The first instances of the Land of the Morning Calm encountering Western civilization occurred along the banks of the Hangang River. Unfortunately, these first meetings were typically ones of conflict. The river functioned as a strategic entry point for accessing the peninsula; it was the primary gateway for foreign powers that sought to penetrate Korea. The initial struggle occurred in 1866, when troops from a French fleet pillaged the fortress on

The Outer Kyujanggak,
the Joseon Dynasty Royal Protocols

Ganghwado Island in retaliation for the execution of French Catholics by the Koreans. In this six-week-long battle, which was to go down in history as the first-ever armed conflict between Korea and a Western power, the French occupied the island for a month and plundered the thousand-plus volumes kept at the Outer Kyujanggak, or royal library, carrying away 359 of them while burning the rest. (The Outer Kyujanggak was built on this island to house the surplus records that could not be stored at the main Kyujanggak at the royal palace in Seoul, which did not have enough room for them.) Following a bilateral agreement at the G20 Summit, Korea received the volumes on temporary loan from the French government for the first time in 145 years. While the loan is temporary and the agreement expires in five years, the volumes are currently in Korea and are being exhibited in various museums around the country.

Ever since then, key conflicts have invariably been fought along the Imjingang River, the entryway to the Hangang. Although the 1866 French invasion of Korea forced the country to come into contact with the outside world for a time, Korea soon reverted to isolationism after the French retreated. However, this isolationism didn't last long, as other external powers continued to arrive at the banks of the Hangang. It was these turn-of-the-century conflicts in the late 19th century that ultimately paved the way for the modernization of Korean society. Subsequent changes in the country have oftentimes occurred along its riverbanks. In the 20th century, the river influenced the fates of many Koreans when then-president

Night view of the Olympicdaegyo Bridge

Syngman Rhee blew up the main bridge to slow North Korean forces from taking over the capital city of Seoul. In these ways and more, the Hangang has directly witnessed the modern transformations undergone by the country. Although much of the drama that unfolded along its banks was a story of tragedy and conflict, the Hangang went on to quietly overlook the progress made by Korea as well. The rapid development and industrialization Korea achieved since the Korean War is encapsulated in the expression "Miracle on the Han," which is often used to describe the economic success Korea achieved within the span of just a few decades.

That is why, to most Koreans, the Hangang is a place of rich significance. It is more than a river; it was along its banks that the country first met the outside world, experienced some of the worst travesties of a fratricidal war, and witnessed unprecedented economic development.

On the Road to Urbanization

In the middle of the 20th century, Seoul started to encroach on the river. With the city's urbanization, even the broad waters of the Hangang could not prevent the spread of development along both banks. In the late 1960s, Seoul formally adopted plans for integrating the river into the city's development, thus starting a process that would drastically alter the river's physical characteristics and natural ecology, while making over its appearance. As a result, the Hangang has become an integral component of Seoul's urban environment.

After the riverside roadways were built, never-ending rows of high-rise apartment complexes started to wall off the river. While this was going on, massive reclamation projects were underway all along the river. The area of Dongbuichon-dong was built up and developed into the Hangang Apartment Complex, while to the south the Apgujeong area was reclaimed, eventually becoming home to the Hyundai Apartment Complex. The reclamation of the Banpo and Jamsil areas proceeded in tandem—the former becoming a large-scale apartment district, the latter a residential neighborhood alongside embankment roads.

Yeouido was once nothing but a sandbank extending out to the middle of the Hangang. As time went by, it was surrounded with dikes and gradually turned into an island. (Bamseom islet, which used to be seen near the white beach at Seogang, is now almost completely submerged.) The Jamsil reclamation project was part of a plan to relocate urban dwellers north of the river to the southern bank. Some 26.4 km² of land in Yeongdong was combined with 13.2 km² of land in Jamsil to form a huge residential district. Within a period of only 20 years or so, the population south of the Hangang started to overtake the population to the north. But the development of the river did not end there. The river underwent another makeover with the Hangang River Comprehensive Development Plan, a mammoth public works project initiated in 1982.

Hangang parks are easily accessible via public transportation.

Ecology Parks

The Hangang River has long been a habitat for aquatic ecology. Like most rivers, it serves as an intersection where aquatic ecology comes into contact with land-based ecology, making it especially environmentally sensitive. However, in the process of Korea's modernization and urbanization, the environment for animal and plant life in downstream areas has faced serious disruption and deterioration. Accordingly, the government has been conducting regular studies of the riverine ecology since 1987 in order to develop measures for its improvement and restoration. In conjunction with these efforts, the government has also sought to create parks along the riverfront in an attempt to both attract visitors to the area and protect the river's wildlife.

The Deer Corral and sculpture garden within Seoul Forest

Seoul Forest (Ttukseom Island)

Officially opened in June 2005 after a year-long development period, the Seoul Forest is the city's very own Central Park or Hyde Park. To offer citizens a big enough place to relax and unwind in the green outdoors, sheltered from sounds of traffic, the city transformed a former sports park into a 1.16 km^2 green space with five thematic micro-parks, one of which is the Ecological Park. Known for its over 40 different species of roses, this park offers visitors a chance to stroll along the river and admire these colorful, intoxicating flowers, while also sighting some fish along the way. While roses are obviously the main attraction at this park located on Ttukseom Island, groves of wetland plant species, including reeds, silver banner grass, and rose-gold pussy willows can also be seen. Various kinds of water plants, such as water chestnut and floating moss, can be found in downstream areas where the waters flow by gently. Along with these sights, Seoul Forest also features an insect garden in its Nature Experiencing Study Field and an outdoor nature classroom for children in its Wetlands Ecological Field.

Nanji Hangang Park

The Nanji Ecological Park, located within Nanji Hangang Park, is an eco-friendly facility and habitat for wild animals. (Students often come here for their nature assignments.) As recently as 50 or so years ago, tigers were known to live in the remote forest areas of the upstream reaches of the Hangang. However, it seems these tigers have since vanished due to the Korean War (1950–1953) and the country's subsequent modernization. But other animals—antelopes, boars, roe deer, wildcats, otters—continue to live there as always, while the downstream mountainous areas are home to a variety of herbivores, including rabbits and elk.

Jamsil Fish Trail

Families who visit Jamsil Fish Trail, or the Jamsil Mulgogi-gil, can delight in watching schools of Hangang fish swim upstream in a four-meter-wide, 228-meter-long ecological channel specially created for this purpose. Located south of the river in the Jamsil area, this trail was built in 2006 and comes equipped with a small park and walkways developed around an "aquatic life" theme. The river's water quality, which deteriorates as it moves downstream, determines the species of fish that can survive in its waters. Throughout the length of the river, some 50 species of fish can be found, of which 20 are unique to Korea. Explanations and pictures of many of these species can be found at the park, offering an educational reason to take the kids there.

Other Ecology Parks

Many ecology-related parks were developed alongside the river as part of an effort that came on the heels of Yeouido Saetgang Ecology Park, which was opened in 1997 as a way to help restore the waterside environment. These newer parks include the Gil-dong Ecology Park, Gangseo Wetland Ecology Park, Godeok-dong Ecology Park, and Seonyudo Park. At the same time, small urban streams, which residents traditionally gave a wide berth to because of their foul odor and filthy waters, are gradually returning to their natural state. After much neglect, the stream of Yangjaecheon was restored to a naturally flowing stream and ecological haven; the fish and insects that had once vacated the premises have since returned, along with thriving communities of ducks and raccoons.

(top) Seonyudo Park
(bottom) Yeouido Saetgang Ecology Park

BEYOND THE "MIRACLE ON THE HAN"

Banghwadaegyo Bridge

While the rapid development of years past helped shape the city into what it is today, new and equally important projects need to be dealt with directly. Over the years, extensive urban development along the river's downstream areas has done serious damage to its natural ecology. Nowadays, automobiles take up nearly every centimeter of the riverside. Both the riverbed and its banks have been artificially straightened. And the fact that both sides of the Hangang are almost completely covered in asphalt and concrete poses a serious problem as well, leading many to worry whether the river has lost its regenerative capacity to sustain aquatic and plant life. To help restore this ecology, the government has designated several ecological preservation areas where public access is prohibited. Due to such efforts, some 25 species of birds, fish, and insects now reside (permanently or during the winter) on the islet of Bamseom, while the wetland areas of Dunchon-dong—practically next door to an apartment complex—is home to 27 thriving species of wetland plants, a rare sight in an urban residential area.

In addition, the island of Nanjido—used for 15 years as a landfill area, and thus despised by neighborhood residents—has been transformed into a public golf course and ecology theme park. Nanji Hangang Park (adjacent to the Sangam-dong World Cup Stadium) serves as a habitat for all sorts of birds, plants and insects. Previously neglected and shunned, Nanjido is now a hands-on ecology classroom for students as well as a welcome place of rest and recreation for the residents of Seoul.

The Hangang has long been an invaluable source of fresh water. Dams were built mainly at its midstream and downstream segments, while large cities and smaller communities were developed along downstream areas. Paldang Dam, in the downstream area, supplies potable water for the 20 million residents of Seoul and its surrounding metropolitan areas.

The reed field of Haneul Park on Nanjido

Yeouido: Seoul's Manhattan

The business successes of Korea's phenomenal economic expansion and the urban development of Seoul came to be known as the "Miracle on the Han." The development of the riverbanks forever altered the face of the city. Since mushrooming in the 1970s, apartment complexes have largely become the standard form of residence in Korea. It is natural enough, then, that the areas along the Hangang River have come to abound with high rises. These apartments first began to appear along the river in 1973, with the construction of apartment projects on Yeouido and along the southern banks. Residential districts with excellent views of the river include Apgujeong-dong (Gangnam-gu), Banpo-dong (Seocho-gu), Heukseok-dong (Dongjak-gu), Jamsil-dong (Songpa-gu), Ichon-dong (Yongsan-gu), and Gwangjang-dong (Gwangjin-gu).

With 63 floors measuring a height of 264 m, the 63 City in Yeouido is Korea's fifth tallest building.

The apartment units along the river are far more expensive than comparable developments in other areas. Part of this has to do with their convenient location, but the view of the river is arguably a more important factor. When developers advertise the sale of units in apartment projects like this, the point that they emphasize most is their view of the Hangang River. Even within a single apartment complex, prices can vary by tens of millions of won (the equivalent of tens of thousands of dollars) depending on the quality of its view of the river—proof positive of the feature's intrinsic value.

Long a derelict island of sand, Yeouido began a rapid transformation in 1968 that would see it becoming a modern-day symbol of the Hangang River. Today, it is home to the National Assembly Building; the KBS, MBC and SBS TV broadcasters; major newspaper publishers; and securities firms. In short, it is the center of Korea's political, media, and financial activities. Accordingly, Yeouido has come to be known as the "Manhattan of Seoul." Few could have imagined that such a desolate site, which housed little more than a plane runway and pasture land until only a few decades ago, would become the center of Korean politics and TV broadcasting as well as the "Wall Street of Korea."

Escaping the Everyday

In addition to being a magnet for residential development, the Hangang River is also popular among those needing an escape from the ordinary. The sight of its gently flowing waters can do wonders for those recovering from a hectic workday or washing away their fatigue and worries. Riverside development may have occurred at a breakneck pace with Seoul's urban growth, but fortunately the riverbanks also offer an economical means of providing park areas and walking paths. On holidays, families flock to the parks along the embankments, while couples enjoy quiet walks along the river's edge. Cyclists, roller-bladers, joggers, and pet-walkers are often

Banpodaegyo Moonlight Rainbow Fountain

found out and about, enjoying their various respective activities. Diverse festivals are staged here all year round with spectacular fireworks displays, making the Hangang a sought-out destination among foreigners as well. Cafés are especially popular, due to the panoramic views they offer of the river and bridges.

A pleasure boat excursion is one delightful way to view the river's magnificent scenery. On a leisurely cruise along the river, you can enjoy the sunlight sparkling on the water during the day and the marvelous city lights at night. If the French poet Guillaume Apollinaire wrote of the elegant beauty of the Pont Mirabeau over

the River Seine, then the poets and painters of Korea have traditionally lauded the bridges across the Hangang, among them Cheonhodaegyo, Jamsildaegyo, Yeongdongdaegyo, Donghodaegyo, Seongsudaegyo, and Hannamdaegyo. These bridges, each which its own character, create an attractive urban scene when illuminated at night.

Those who seek a more thrilling experience have the option of speeding along the river in a motorboat, leaving a spray of water in their wake. The pleasure boats can be boarded at Jamsil, Yeouido, Yanghwa, and Nanji, where six ferry routes are available. Each of the ferry landings houses a floating restaurant, enabling patrons to take in the scenery and atmosphere of the Hangang. There are also many floating lounge bars to be found along the river, where patrons can curl up with a cocktail and relax to the sounds of live jazz.

Yeouido Hangang Park

Hangang River by Districts

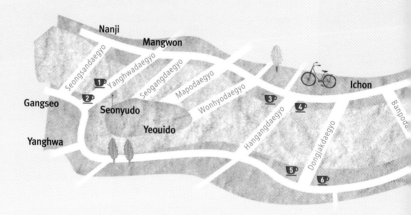

Nanji

Mangwon

Seongsandaegyo

Yanghwadaegyo

Seogangdaegyo

Mapodaegyo

Wonhyodaegyo

Hangangdaegyo

Dongjakdaegyo

Banpod...

Ichon

Gangseo

Seonyudo

Yeouido

Yanghwa

Cafés on the Hangang River

Seoul's nightscape is pretty fantastic. Even the most jaded of city dwellers will feel a tug at his or her heartstrings upon looking up from a nighttime cab ride home and seeing the dusk lights settling over the Hangang River. The many cafés and observatories located along six of the river's 31 bridges take full advantage of this view.

☕ Riverside Cafés

1. Aritaum Seonyu
2. Aritaum Yanghwa
3. Café Nodeul
4. Café Rio
5. Café Sunset
6. Café Cloud
7. Coffee Marina
8. Hannam Saemal Café
9. J-bug
10. Riverview 8th Ave.
11. Jamsil Maru Café

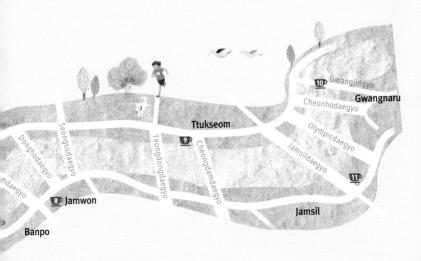

Dongjakdaegyo Bridge

The twin establishment Café Cloud and Café Sunset on Dongjakdaegyo Bridge have the highest observation decks, standing five stories tall. The river flows right underneath, giving one the sensation of being on board a cruise ship. Because of the striking night views, photographers are often found here, competing with starry-eyed lovebirds for a good seat.

Yanghwadaegyo Bridge

Cafe Aritaum Yanghwa and Seonyu on Yanghwadaegyo Bridge are unmistakable for their shape, resembling *origami* paper cranes. Seonyudo Park, a riverfront ecological facility, is located nearby and can be seen from Café Seonyu, while neighboring Yanghwa offers a distant view of the National Assembly Building, Korea's parliament. These two cafés have unassuming façades and are both one-story buildings.

Hangangdaegyo Bridge

Cafe Nodeul and Cafe Rio, located on Hangangdaegyo Bridge, are popular with the younger crowd, who come here for the chic décor. From here, you can look out at the famous 63 Building, Mt. Namsan, and Mt. Bukhansan. There are bicycle ramps for enthusiasts, and a soccer field is located nearby.

2

Chapter Two

THREE MAJOR MOUNTAINS

People have traditionally described the shape of the Korean Peninsula as a tiger, its backbone traced by the Baekdu-daegan Mountain Range, which runs from Mt. Baekdusan in the north to Mt. Jirisan in the south. This range has been thought by many Koreans to be the country's buttress and spiritual touchstone. The mountains have spawned religious thought as well, as represented by the Sanshin, or mountain god, who is said to reign supreme over the earthly world. This might not be much of an exaggeration— mountains (or at the very least jutting hills) can be seen from virtually anywhere in the country. With over 70% of the territory covered by mountains, it's no surprise then that many Koreans enjoy hiking and strolling along the footpaths. The three most distinctive mountains (all, obviously, part of the Baekdu-daegan) are Mt. Bukhansan, Mt. Jirisan, and Mt. Seoraksan.

MT. BUKHANSAN: SEOUL'S STRONGHOLD

Mt. Bukhansan, the most representative mountain of the nation's capital, functions as a "power plant" that supplies an energetic life force to the other mountains around Seoul. According to feng shui (*pungsujiri* in Korean), the mountains that ring Seoul on all sides create an especially propitious site. In the early Joseon period, Seoul was developed according to the principles of *pungsujiri*. From the city's standpoint, the most critical mountains are Mt. Bugaksan and Mt. Bukhansan. In *pungsujiri*, it is important to have *hyeol* (points where the energies of the land converge) in the front, but it is even more essential to have a primary mountain supporting the site from the rear. Seoul is well-positioned to receive the life force emanating from the mountain range that runs from Mt. Baekdusan to the Hanbukjeongmaek range. It was for this propitious setting that Yi Seonggye, founder of the Joseon Dynasty (1392–1910), selected Seoul as the site of his new capital.

Clear skies above Seoul, as seen from Mt. Bukhansan

With its intriguingly shaped cliff formations and precipitous peaks, Mt. Bukhansan has traditionally been a strategic area for the defense of the capital city of Seoul. Not surprisingly, people say that there has been a fortress in the mountains for as long as anyone can remember. The current Bukhansanseong fortress was built in 1711 by King Sukjong at the recommendation of his court and military advisors. Taking full advantage of the mountain's rugged topography, the fortress was designed to defend the capital against invasions from the north. Mt. Bukhansan is also known as Mt. Samgaksan or "three-horns mountain," because the profile of its three main peaks (Baegundae, Insubong, and Mangyeongdae) resembles three horns when viewed from a distance.

As for the citizens of the Seoul metropolitan area, they are indeed blessed to have this wondrous mountain located so close by. To truly enjoy this blessing, however, it is necessary to make the effort to climb up its granite cliffs. Unlike the long-ago days of the Joseon Dynasty, it is now possible to reach the entrance by bus or subway from anywhere in Seoul in about an hour. This convenient proximity means that in Seoul it is possible to cross from the mundane world to the divine realm of the gods in a mere 60 minutes. When you enter Mt. Bukhansan, don't come with your mind full of burdens from the secular world—the mountain will reject those whose backpacks are filled with lingering traces of city life.

Mt. Bukhansan National Park, which encompasses Mt. Bukhansan and Mt. Dobongsan, attracts some 8.5 million visitors each year. This is the highest visitor count among all of the 20 national parks in Korea, beating out even Mt. Seoraksan and Mt. Jirisan. The ranks of those climbing the slopes of Mt. Bukhansan include former presidents, as well as politicians, scholars, writers, and painters.

The first people to roam Mt. Bukhansan were no doubt the hunters and gatherers of medicinal herbs who settled nearby. Up

Mountaineer Um Hong-gil and his fellows are hiking Mt. Bukhansan.

until the Joseon Dynasty, the mountain was home to a wide variety of animals—including tigers, which were often spotted on the slopes of Mt. Inwangsan, the southernmost point of Mt. Bukhansan, in the vicinity of Gyeongbokgung Palace. As recently as 10 years ago, so much plant life flourished on the mountain that people would occasionally stumble upon rare wild ginseng there.

Nowadays, the areas at the base of Mt. Bukhansan and Mt. Dobongsan have undergone a dramatic transformation. Shops specializing in hiking gear (like those previously congregating in the Namdaemun and Dongdaemun markets) began opening in this area. With the steady stream of visitors drawn by the mountain, retails enjoy brisk sales on any given day of the week, and especially on weekends. Convenience stores, ATMs, and bathhouses can all be found at the foot of the mountain, along with a variety of restaurants serving food to satisfy the palates of all hikers. A visit to Mt. Bukhansan is also an opportunity to view the latest mountaineering brands and styles from all over the world. When visiting Korea a few years ago, Harish Kafadia, the former vice president of the Indian Mountaineering Foundation, was so impressed with the quality of the clothing and gear on the hordes of Mt. Bukhansan climbers that he asked the Korean hikers accompanying him, "Are all these people preparing for an expedition to the Himalayas?" (In fact, Korea is the only country in the world that has produced three climbers who have conquered all 14 peaks of the Himalayas that measure over 8,000 meters in height: Um Hong-gil, Park Young-seok, and Han Wang-ryong.)

TEMPLE STAYS

Imagine escaping the city to a quiet temple in the mountains, where the only sounds accompanying your thoughts are the clear notes of a *moktak* (wooden gong). Imagine waking before daybreak and being greeted by utter stillness. Imagine three meals a day of humble yet healthy fare, full of fresh-picked vegetables and fluffy white rice, alongside a wooden bowl of warm soup (*sans* meat or garlic or onions—none of the so-called pungent foods that can distract the Buddhist practitioner).

Temple stays, as these escapes are known, are more than your average New Age R&R retreats; some are infamous for being demanding. They are open to everyone, practicing Buddhists and non-believers alike. Scheduling is surprisingly flexible; fervent adherents may stay for months, while tentative first-timers can devote just one afternoon of their time. Depending on the temple, participants may find themselves either in a small group or in a large hall surrounded by dozens of fellow soul-searchers. The average day begins at 3 or 4 a.m. Participants are roused from their slumber by an alarm, or the low humming of a Buddhist monk in lieu of a wake-up call. Programs vary by temple, but almost all of them require participants to partake in prostrations before the Buddha—108 in total, a number denoting the collective mental sufferings experienced by one individual in his past, present, and future lives.

Participants can also take walks through the temple grounds or sit down with the guiding monk to hear tales of his life and the knowledge he has acquired. Activities such as handicrafts and tea ceremonies are also offered. Golgusa Temple is popular for its location (near the historic city of Gyeongju), while Haeinsa is famous for its legacy; for the Seoul visitor, there's the urban temple of Bongeunsa in Gangnam's Samseong-dong.

MT. JIRISAN: A WARM EMBRACE

Arguably the most beloved mountain in Korea, Mt. Jirisan is located in Korea's southern region, where the Baekdu-daegan mountain range ends. It is particularly renowned for its scenic beauty: Korea enjoys all four seasons, and their respective characteristics can be felt all around in the mountain's flora and fauna. Over 3 million people visit each year to revel in this beauty.

Located in eponymous Jirisan National Park, Mt. Jirisan is home to nearly 5,000 species of animals and wildlife. Given its climate, the vegetation here ranges from warm-temperature plants to temperate central forest and cold forest. Animals—hares, wildcats, and deer among them—can often be seen scampering through the forest. This was the first national park designated by the government in 1967, and it is still the largest, stretching across three provincial jurisdictions.

Elecampane   Dogtooth violet   Cornelian cherry   Flying squirrel

Temples in Jirisan

The "ji" in the name "Jirisan" comes from a Chinese character meaning "wisdom"; not surprisingly, the area is known for its famous temples, and the visitors who pass through the temple doors. Seven major Buddhist temples are scattered around Mt.

Hwaeomsa Temple

Jirisan, perhaps the most famous of them being Hwaeomsa Temple, which is also the largest temple on Mt. Jirisan and home to four national treasures. One noteworthy feature is the stone art, including the Gakhwangjeon (National Treasure No. 67), a three-story stone pagoda buttressed by four lions at its base, and the Gakhwangjeon Seokdeung, one of the largest stone lanterns in existence. The temple, which is situated near Jirisan's Nogodan peak, was built by the Buddhist master Yeongidaesa in the fifth year of the reign of King Jinheung of Silla (544 CE), a few centuries after the introduction of Buddhism to Korea. However, it was badly destroyed during the Japanese invasion near the end of the sixteenth century, and subsequently restored during the reign of King Injo of Joseon (1630).

Seomjingang River Maehwa Village

Ssanggyesa Temple is located in the middle of southern Jirisan. Built about 1,300 years ago, it was also destroyed during the Japanese invasion before later being reconstructed by Jingamseonsa when he rebuilt Hwaeomsa Temple. Another temple, Beopgyesa, stands at 1,450 meters above sea level and boasts perhaps the highest altitude of any temple in Korea. Getting there requires a roughly two-hour trek. Beopgyesa Temple has endured the trials and tribulations of Korean history: it suffered a severe fire that was set by the Japanese as they fled the mountain from an attack by General Yi Seonggye in 1380, as well as another set in 1908 to punish anti-Japanese guerillas hiding out in the mountainous terrain. In 1948, the temple was occupied by counterinsurgencies; once again, fire was set to the area to force the rebels to flee. Yet despite the many fires and the harassment, the temple was always diligently rebuilt.

Return to Farming

Along with followers of the Buddhist faith, Mt. Jirisan has also become a favorite destination for former urbanites who gave up life in the city to move to the mountain and take up a more unhurried, organic lifestyle. Known in Korea as the *gwinong* ("return to farming") lifestyle, this trend has been more and more enthusiastically embraced of late, especially by younger couples in their thirties and forties who move to the mountain foothills, often with their children in tow. Farming classes are now widely available for those wanting to learn how to till their own soil and grow their own vegetables. While there have been some reported cases of residents giving up and returning to the city once they realize how heavy the burdens of field labor can be, in many cases, the residents report more fulfillment and satisfaction, deriving joy from their improved quality of life.

Painful History

As important as Mt. Jirisan's beauty and cultural significance are, its place in history warrants mention as well, for it bore witness to one of the most tumultuous times in Korean modern history. Following the withdrawal of Japanese troops in 1945, ideological differences tore the country apart, with formerly anti-Japanese protesters teaming with leftists to call for the punishment of the pro-Japanese establishment and demanding that land be redistributed to the people. When a mass uprising in October 1946 failed, the survivors were forced to flee to the mountains, most notably Mt. Jirisan. From then until 1953, the Rhee Syngman administration had the mountain surrounded, arresting whomever they could capture and slowly letting the rest of the rebels wither away. This painful chapter in Korean history has been dramatized in various forms of popular culture and is still remembered by Koreans to this day.

Ten Scenic Views of Mt. Jirisan

Topping out at 1,915 meters above sea level, Mt. Jirisan is famed for its 10 scenic views, which are 1) the sunrise from Cheonwangbong, possibly the best site to watch the sunrise in Korea and a popular destination for people hankering to watch the New Year sunrise on December 31; 2) the Nogodan sea of clouds, from where one can see a blanket of clouds below one's feet; 3) the sunset from Banyabong; 4) the full moon at Byuksoryeong, 5) the crisp autumn leaves of Piagol forest, host of the annual Autumn Leaves Festival; 6) royal azalea blossoms covering the Royal Azalea Plateau some 1,200 meters up on Mt. Jirisan; 7) the Chilseondong Valley, supposedly home to seven mountain gods; 8) the Seomjincheongryu, meaning the "silky flow of the Seomjingang River"; 9) the 60-meter-high Buril waterfall between Cheonghakbong and Baekhakbong; and 10) the red sunset seen through the mountain haze (known in Korean as "Yeonhasungyeong").

Seomjingang River

Royal Azalea Plateau, Piagol forest, The Chilseon Valley, The Nogodan sea of clouds
(clockwise from top left)

MT. SEORAKSAN: KOREA'S SPIRITUAL TOUCHSTONE

If Mt. Bukhansan is distinct for being the highest mountain in the capital city and Mt. Jirisan is beloved by Koreans for its warmer breezes and rich golden hues, then Mt. Seoraksan, or "snowy crags mountain," stands proud in its steep grandeur. Nestled in Seoraksan National Park in northern Korea's Gangwon-do Province, it is the third highest mountain in South Korea, after Mt. Hallasan (located on Jeju-do Island) and Mt. Jirisan. Mt. Seoraksan's highest peak is Daecheongbong, at 1,708 meters above sea level. The park was designated a natural monument in 1965, and later expanded in 1970 into a 354.6-km^2 nature reserve that includes 28 peaks, 58 valleys, two hot springs, and 12 Buddhist temples.

The entire mountain was designated by UNESCO as a Biosphere Preservation District in 1982. Since then, buses and other means of transportation have been granted only limited access to the park grounds. With all these measures in place to protect the area around Mt. Seoraksan, it is no wonder that the park is rich in biodiversity, and the park authorities have established further special protection zones for particular species. Of these, the dwarf stone pine (*Pinus pumila*) is noteworthy for being found nowhere else in Korea. These trees are exceedingly rare and under a growing threat from changes in the climate. Among the local fauna, the long-tailed goral (*Nemorhaedus caudatus*) is also found in the mountainous areas of Siberia and Manchuria. This species is quite rare, and it is a treat for an unassuming hiker to stumble upon one of these mammals on the mountain.

(top) Verdure of the Inner Seorak
(bottom) Winter landscape of Mt. Seoraksan

Along with these rare species, the forests of Mt. Seoraksan are also rich and colorful, containing both deciduous trees and evergreens. Nearly 1,000 different species of plants, 90 species of birds, 360 species of insects, and 40 species of freshwater fish dwell here. The majestic rock formations of Mt. Seoraksan are worth noting, among them the Ulsanbawi rock mountain, with six jagged peaks stretching for four kilometers in circumference. A cute folk legend has it that this rock traveled north to represent the southern city of Ulsan as part of Mt. Geumgangsan, only to see that it arrived too late. Embarrassed, it began to slink back south, but fell asleep near the Seorak region. Upon waking up, it decided to stay because of the beauty of the place.

Visiting Seoraksan

Mt. Seoraksan is a favored destination for "temple stayers," those who visit Buddhist temples for the cultural experience to seek spiritual fulfillment or enjoy a short break from the fast-paced life of the city. Particularly noteworthy is Sinheungsa Temple, the head temple of the Jogye Order of Korean Buddhism. Heading some 40 branch temples in Gangwon-do Province, the temple boasts a long history, having first been built in the year 652 during the reign of Queen Jindeok of the Silla Dynasty. Baekdamsa Temple, another popular spot to visit, was built by the same architect responsible for Sinheungsa Temple—the Buddhist master Jajang.

While some come to Mt. Seoraksan in the hope of achieving spiritual enlightenment, the vast majority of visitors to this mountain and its surrounding areas come for the more earthly delights, namely the gorgeous natural beauty of the park. Autumn in particular sees many visitors coming for the rich red and yellow foliage covering the mountain peaks. In the summer monsoon season, the streams meandering through the mountain can swell, leading to dangerous accidents. In all the other seasons, however,

Tottering rock

there's nothing to stop visitors from enjoying one of the many nature walks and hiking trails planned along the mountain's slopes.

Outer and Inner Seorak

Visitors have easy access to the Outer Seorak section of the national park, which is where the Sinheungsa Temple is located, along with the popular Heundeulbawi or "tottering rock," which has yet to fall down the edge of the cliff where it's located, despite many visitors' strained attempts. This section is also home to the Biryong ("flying dragon") falls, where the waters crashing over the rocks are said to look much like dragons flying up to the skies. Gwongeumseong, the ruins of a fortress built during the reign of King Gojong in the Goryeo Dynasty, is also located in Outer Seorak. Legend has it that two generals with the last names of Gwon and Geum built the castle in one night to protect their families from a Mongolian invasion—hence the fortress's name. The climb is steep to get to the fortress, but the view from the top is well worth it. The main entrance to the park itself is only fifteen minutes away from the city of Sokcho.

Inner Seorak can only be reached by a long climb—8.5 kilometers, to be exact. This section of the park is where Baekdamsa Temple is located, as well as the 88-meter-high Daeseungpokpo Waterfall, so the fruits are well worth the labors. Various walking trails offer visitors the chance to trek to destinations such as Baekdam Valley and Baegundong Valley. The

trails are well marked and quite safe, so it's difficult to get lost. Daeseungpokpo, a favorite relaxation spot of King Gyeongseon, the last king of Silla, and the Naerincheon, the only stream in Korea that flows north (like the Nile), are also located in Inner Seorak. While these parts are obviously less accessible than Outer Seorak, they are also that much more tranquil, which is why a growing number of visitors brave the climb to admire the mountain's waterfalls and distinctive valleys.

1. Dinosaur Ridge
2. Buddha, Sinheungsa Temple
3. Seorak-dong village

3
Chapter Three

SURROUNDED ON THREE SIDES BY SEA

The sea: the cradle of life for all things on earth. Like a mother's womb, it nurtured life forms, allowing the Earth to gradually evolve into a vibrant planet where an abundance of plant and animal life would flourish. In that respect, the Korean Peninsula, surrounded as it is by the nurturing sea on three sides, is truly blessed by nature.

The Korean people have long had a close relationship with the sea, which was revered as a bountiful food source. Ancient shell mounds show that the Koreans who settled near coastal areas survived on the shellfish that was readily available along the shoreline. Prehistoric rock carvings found at Bangudae in Ulsan's Daegok-ri village also depict whales and other marine life, suggesting an abundance of fishery resources.

Each of the seas that surround the Korean Peninsula to the south, east, and west has its own distinctive characteristics. The daily lives and livelihoods of the fishermen on the three coasts also differ somewhat. On the east coast, where the roads are generally in better condition, their life is simple and monotonous. The rugged coastlines, rocky roads, and expansive tidal flats that characterize the western and southern coasts are reflected in the endless ups and downs of local residents. Despite the different traits, one thing is common to them all—the longstanding significance of the sea in the lives of Koreans.

A HISTORY ON THE OCEAN

Neither especially expansive nor narrow, the seas surrounding Korea have bustled with maritime activity since prehistoric times. Many Koreans settled along the country's shores to enjoy the benefits of the sea's plentiful resources. Given Korea's geographical status as a peninsula, however, the country was often subjected to heavy foreign invasion as well, especially from neighboring countries like Japan and China. So it was in the years from 1592 to

Chuam Beach near the East Sea

Geobukseon (Turtle Ship) mockup in Yeosu

1598 that Joseon had to defend itself against a large-scale Japanese military offensive on both land and sea. It was able to repel the invaders thanks to the heroics of the legendary Admiral Yi Sun-sin (1545–1598)—whose stunning 23 victories in 23 naval battles gave rise to his legend of invincibility—and his vaunted Turtle Ship. But Joseon failed to maintain its maritime prowess after the war, and eventually was forced to yield to Japan's naval power and open its ports. Relations between the two countries have been shaped by the Koreans who used sea routes to reach and settle in Japan, where they eventually came to exert political influence on its early national development.

Overland Routes, Sea Routes

In modern times, maritime capabilities have been critical in shaping the power relationships of East Asia. When World War II ended, the sea routes that linked up East Asia were shut down, preventing the "East Asian Mediterranean" from playing its intermediary role. Over time, the region's structure was realigned. Today, Korea maintains a maritime network that is connected to all regions and nations of East Asia in terms of trade and cultural exchange. On this foundation, and with assured access to key international sea lanes, Korea is well positioned to reap tremendous gains— economically, diplomatically, and culturally—from its maritime capabilities. The country has, for example, laid claim to its status as the world's number one shipbuilder. According to industry data compiled by Clarkson, a market research firm that specializes in shipbuilding and commercial shipping, Korea's shipbuilding industry was the largest producer in the world in 2005, with an output of 14.5 million compensated gross tons (CGT) of vessels, compared to 7 million from China and 6.2 million from Japan.

WEST SEA:
THE RICH TIDAL FLATS OF THE YELLOW SEA

Situated between Korea and China, the West Sea has shallow waters, their depth averaging just 40 meters. Also known as the Yellow Sea or East China Sea, it is where the major rivers of China and Korea deposit their silty, mostly yellow sand, giving the water a yellowish tinge, from which the name Yellow Sea is derived. If the East Sea is known for its depth and the South Sea for its sandy beaches, then the West Sea is known for its tidal flats. The western

Mallipo Beach

coastline of Korea has a complex shape that includes many islands, miniature "peninsulas," and cozy beaches tucked into unexpected corners.

Taean-gun County (also known as Taean Bando, or Taean Peninsula), juts out to the west on a small peninsula. This county alone is home to more than 30 beaches, one of them—Mallipo—home to hundreds of species of flora. Although the site has seen a drop in tourism following an oil spill in 2007 (a crane barge collision sent over 10,000 tons of oil pouring into the sea, laying waste to much of the sea's ecosystem), Taean-gun nevertheless remains a much-loved attraction for many visitors who come to appreciate the view and the ecological merits of the region, especially its beautiful tidal flats. Another prominent place on the West Sea is Incheon, home to Incheon International Airport, which acts as the gateway for most visitors to Korea.

The extreme tidal variations along the western coast are responsible for the vast stretches of tidal flats. In fact, the tidal basins in Korea rank among the five largest in the world (along with those of the eastern coast of Canada, the eastern coast of the United States, the North Sea coastline, and the mouth of the Amazon River in Brazil). The tidal flats provide an ideal breeding ground and habitat for marine creatures, and they positively teem with life. They are a paradise for those hoping to harvest a variety of clams and shellfish, while the waters abound in octopuses, yellow croakers, hairtails, anchovies, and blue crabs.

In addition to being a fertile habitat for marine life, the tidal flats have historically been indispensable as a natural filter that cleanses seawater. By filtering out pollutants brought in by the tidal currents, as well as contaminants carried in river waters, the flats purify the waters of the ocean, earning them the nickname of "kidneys of the Earth." The benefits they provide are numerous: serving as a habitat for various maritime species, purifying incoming and outgoing waters, maintaining an ecological balance, stabilizing the weather, and attracting visitors as a tourist destination. Indeed, the tidal flats are essential for our survival.

But since the latter half of the 1980s, various areas have been reclaimed for commercial development. Thus far, some 620 km² s of land have been reclaimed—an area about the size of Seoul city. The development of tidal flats began in the 1960s and 1970s before reaching a peak in the 1980s. Due to these land reclamation projects, Korea's tidal flats have shrunk by about 30 to 40 percent over the past 10 years. The Saemangeum Seawall, in

Saemangeum Seawall

particular, is the world's longest manmade dike, measuring in at nearly 33 km long. Announced as a public project in 1991 by the government, the dike was constructed along the southwest coast of the peninsula, near the city of Gunsan. It was built to create 40,100 hectares of arable land and freshwater lakes, with government plans to turn the surrounding area into a complex for industry, leisure, and green business by 2020.

But with the economic value of tidal flats being as much as 100 times greater than that of farmland and 40 times that of coastal areas, it is now more important than ever to preserve the remaining tidal flats and promote coexistence between people and our natural environment.

EAST SEA: DEEP WATERS, NEW HOPE

The East Sea lies between Korea and Japan and contains the deepest waters anywhere around Korea, reaching 4,000 meters in depth. The average depth of the East Sea is 1,684 m. Warm and cold currents converge here, forming prime fishing grounds. In the fall,

when the North Korean Cold Current is flowing strongly, coldwater fish like walleye pollack and Pacific cod gather in this area to lay their eggs. The cold waters are also conducive to the flourishing of seaweeds such as sea mustard and kelp. In the summer, when the East Korean Warm Current arrives from the south, warmwater species of squid, mackerel, and saury abound.

Several types of whales reside in the East Sea. Among the species that have been caught or known to pass through are the blue whale, fin whale, sei whale, Bryde's whale, minke whale, humpback whale, gray whale, sperm whale, and killer whale. Risso's dolphin and the Pacific white-sided dolphin can be seen as well. For a long time, whales were not a common sight in the area, but their numbers have been on the rise after the institution of a whaling ban in 1985. If you traverse the East Sea by boat, you may also come across some playful dolphins that seem to be looking for new buddies.

Dokdo Island

The East Sea is home to the Dokdo islets, which mark the easternmost point of Korean territory. Dokdo consists of an eastern islet, Dongdo, and a western islet, Seodo, as well as several rocky outcroppings. Its natural scenery includes sea caves carved by ceaseless wave action, along with a variety of spectacular underwater sights. Its marine environment—well preserved thanks to the area's lack of human contact—is inhabited by more than 100 species of fish, including rockfish, black rockfish, bulge-headed wrasse, and rock bream. Dokdo is also known for its plentiful supply of abalone and sea cucumber. Although it is located fairly far north (37°14′), the Tsushima Warm Current makes its environment suitable for fish that are usually found in subtropical waters. For example, the neon damsel, which thrives in tropical and subtropical waters like those around Jeju-do, will make its way north to Dokdo in the summer.

To Koreans, the East Sea has always symbolized hope and a new beginning, as the east is the direction from which the sun rises. On New Year's Day, hordes of people go to visit notable attractions on the coast, where they can best get a glimpse of the first sunrise of the year—many having driven for hours from different regions of

Korea to stake out the best spot. As the sun casts its golden glow over their faces, the throngs crowding the cliffs look up at the sky and utter a silent prayer. Some of the more popular locations are Gyeongpodae Beach (the largest beach on the east coast) and Jeongdongjin Beach, which sits right outside the Jeongdongjin Train Station and offers a refreshing view of the sunrise.

SOUTH SEA: MANY ISLANDS, MANY FLAVORS

The South Sea waters are somewhat deeper than those of the Yellow Sea, but their maximum depth of 200 meters is nowhere near the reaches of the East Sea. The southern coastline's rugged topography and the countless islands and islets scattered about the offshore waters create a gorgeous seascape and give the sea its nickname, "Sea of Many Islands."

There's Gageo-do Island, located farthest away from the southernmost coast of the western peninsula. Also known as Soheuksan-do, Gageo-do Island is a magnificent sight, with cliffs of intriguing shapes creating a unique complement to a sea so dark it looks black. First-time visitors to the island are often mesmerized by its enchanting beauty. Another highlight is Geomun-do Island, which is located about two and a half hours from Yeosu by boat and forms part of the Dadohae Maritime National Park, where uninhabited rock pinnacles form a somber yet darkly beautiful sight. Geoje-do Island is historically significant, as it is where Admiral Yi Sun-shin fought the Japanese in the Okpodaecheop, one of the battles of the Imjinwaeran Invasions. The South Sea is also home to Hallyeohaesang National Park, which includes the Hallyeosudo, a waterway that meanders around over 100 islands. Whether visited individually or glimpsed from a distance, as from the Hallyeosudo, the islands of the South Sea are natural wonders, and crowds of visitors flock to this coast annually.

The southern coast also boasts a combination of tidal flats, sandy beaches, and rocky cliffs, providing diverse habitats for various forms of marine life. Influenced by the Kuroshio Current, the water is warm and marked with high salinity, providing a suitable environment for numerous species of brightly colored warm-current fish that thrive in tropical or subtropical waters. The major fish species in the South Sea waters include mackerel, Spanish mackerel, jack mackerel, amberjack, and anchovy. A variety of marine life that favors warm, tropical waters can be found here. The clean, flowing waters are also suitable for the cultivation of oysters, sea squirts, and laver. Because of this abundance of marine life, many quaint fishing villages dot the southern coast, and local residents have developed a distinctive cuisine that revolves around fish, shellfish, and seaweed.

Somaemul-do Island of Tongyeong

FOOD & LIFESTYLE

Seafood

There are many villages in Korea where long-cherished recipes have been handed down from generation to generation. In the southern regions in particular, where the climate is relatively warm, the food is seasoned with pickled seafood, peppers, and spices, which give the food a distinctly spicy, salty, and pungent taste. Some of the more famous recipes from the south (known as "Namdo food") include salted dried octopus, various forms of *jeotgal* (salted/pickled seafood), and *hongtaksamhap*, a combination of fermented thornback, boiled pork, and sour kimchi—not for the faint of heart.

Hoe (top)
Dried cuttlefish (bottom)

Visit any beach along the coast of Korea and you'll find it hard to miss the rows upon rows of raw fish (*hoe*) restaurants open for business, each with its own tanks teeming with live fish. Similar to Japanese sashimi, *hoe* is typically enjoyed with soy sauce (*ganjang*) or sweet-and-spicy *chogochujang*, a derivative of the pepper paste known as *gochujang*—all wrapped in lettuce, with perhaps a clove of raw garlic thrown in for good measure, and popped straight into one's mouth.

Photographs of Korea's shores often display rows of wooden racks where fish or cuttlefish are hung out to dry in the hardy coastal winds. Alongside dried sardines or small anchovies (*myeolchi*), dried cuttlefish constitutes a primary side dish in Korean culinary culture. In addition to salting and pickling, drying seafood was a strategy Koreans used for generations to store food more effectively for upcoming winters, or for periods that would not be particularly conducive to foraging for food. While salted and pickled seafood has enough flavor to pack one big, pungent punch on its own, dried seafood may be considered more bland to the average Korean palate, which is why it is often accompanied by the ubiquitous *gochujang*.

Tenacity and Resilience

Village rites, women divers, tidal flats, stouthearted fishermen—these are some of the prominent characteristics of Korea's fishing villages. People here have experienced pleasure and sorrow for generation after generation in their pursuit of coexistence with the indomitable and tumultuous sea.

The traditional ways of life of Korea fishermen are reflected in their religion, customs, and recreation, which can still be seen today in fishing villages. The culture of fishing villages reveals what Korean fishermen have strived for, how they have lived, and what their attitude toward life is. A good example is the fishermen's ritual to the god of the sea—this has been developed into a unique cultural practice, varying under the influence of geographical conditions and regional customs.

Anyone who builds a house and lives by the sea must be willing to experience life's ups and downs. The currents are relentless and the threat of a tidal wave might be ever-present, but at any moment the sea can change, offering hope instead of despair. The image of the sea that we hold in our hearts is not of a fearsome threat, but of a gentle and generous source of life and dreams. For city and highland residents, the sea is always beautiful, romantic, and heart-rending. But those whose livelihood depends on it must adopt a lifestyle based on tenacity and resilience.

THE DRAGON KING

The dragon king is the archetypical deity representing Korean feelings about the seas. Coastal dwellers believed that the dragon king decided not just their livelihood but their very existence, so they worked to ensure his veneration and appeasement. Fishermen worshipped him in their homes, on their boats, and at village shrines, praying for their safety and an abundant catch, while regularly arranging for shamans to perform highly elaborate rituals in his honor.

The rite to the dragon king

Due to the close bond between the Korean people and the sea, the influences of the dragon king can be readily seen in traditional thought and culture. The deity appears in mythical tales like the story of Shim Chong, which teaches children the practice of filial devotion (*hyo* in Korean). In the tale, the dragon king is instrumental in allowing Shim Chong to be reunited with her blind father. Yet he was not always associated with such virtuous ideals. The most beautiful woman in Korea was said to be Lady Suro, the wife of Lord Sunjeong, who lived during the Silla Dynasty. Legend holds that the dragon king coveted and eventually abducted her, spiriting her off to his dragon palace. He later returned her after being threatened by the Silla people, though not before showing his secular, almost humanlike desires.

In Korea's foundation myths, the kings who founded states were generally described as descendants of the god of heaven, but some were also children of the dragon king. Gyeon Hwon, who founded Later Baekje, was said to be the son of a dragon king, while the grandmother of Wang Geon, founder of Goryeo, was reportedly the daughter of one. It is noteworthy that these myths about children of the dragon king all originated in southwestern Korea—a region that has been actively involved in maritime trade with China and Southeast Asia since prehistoric times.

Chapter Four

RICH WETLANDS

As principal sources of aquatic life and rich treasure troves of biodiversity, wetlands have become ever more in need of protection in the era of climate change. As their name indicates, wetlands are land areas that are basically saturated with water. As thick mud deposits build, they spawn a distinct ecosystem that cannot easily be found elsewhere. The resulting habitat positively teems with life. Microorganisms break down animal waste, preventing the collected water from turning fetid and increasing the water's nutrient content. Wetlands are marvelous models of integrated ecosystems, with awe-inspiring biodiversity. However, constant land development and resource mismanagement have placed them under increasing threat.

Korea's wetlands—inland, coastal, and manmade—are being increasingly encroached upon. The inland ones in particular have become very limited due to land development, although the coastal ones along the West Sea still remain as valued treasures. Korea's topography and climate are such that there aren't many plateau wetlands located on mountaintops, but there are many low-lying wetlands scattered along the streams. If rice paddies are considered manmade wetlands in their own right, then Korea's vast stretches of rice paddies can arguably be called the biggest wetlands in Korea. Apart from these paddies, however, manmade wetlands are few and far between. We discuss coastal wetlands in greater detail in the chapter on Korea's seas, but for now let's take a look at Korea's inland wetlands.

KOREA'S WETLANDS
FIVE WETLANDS, FIVE COLORS

Since adopting the Ramsar Convention (an international treaty, named for the town of Ramsar, Iran, that seeks to raise awareness of wetlands conservation) in 1997, and especially since hosting the

Prickly water lily

2008 Conference of the Contracting Parties, Korea has strived to conserve its many wetlands. The hosting of this conference also led to a tourism boom in the 11 Korean wetlands currently registered under the convention. These sites are true blessings, each with its own ecological character and value. According to wetland specialists, the most environmentally significant areas include the Yongneup High Moor on Mt. Daeamsan, where legend has it that a dragon rested before making its journey to heaven; the Jangdo Island High Moor, which proves wetlands are valuable water resources; Suncheon Bay, a favored rest area among migratory birds such as the hooded crane; and the Ganghwa Maehwamareum Habitat, Korea's first rice paddy wetlands to earn protection status. As mentioned above, these are all inland wetlands.

The Yongneup High Moor

The Yongneup High Moor was the first site in Korea to be registered under Ramsar. Situated within the demilitarized zone (DMZ) near the summit of Mt. Daeamsan, the area is remote and not readily accessible to the general public. The climate on the 1,304-meter mountain is cool and foggy, with temperatures falling below 0°C for five months out of the year and foggy conditions persisting for about half the year. The water that gathers in its summit basin does not readily evaporate, creating conditions ripe for a wetland ecosystem. It is estimated that Yongneup was formed some 4,500 to 5,000 years ago. It drew international attention in the early 1970s when it was the subject of a joint ecological survey conducted by a team of Korean and international scholars on selected sites within the DMZ. Due to its environmental value, the site has been designated a natural monument. In an acidic moor, dead plants decompose at a slower rate, forming a spongy layer of turf that turns acidic when combined with water. Insect-eating plants (such as the round-leaved sundew and the yellowish-white

The Yongneup High Moor in spring

bladderwort) thrive here in the High Moor. These mountain wetland plants supplement the scarce nutrients of the acidic soil as they consume insect life. Twelve species previously unknown in Korea, such as the Grapholita dimorpha moth, have also been discovered—further proof of the High Moor's ability to promote ecological diversity.

The Jangdo Island High Moor

Located in Sinan, Jeollanam-do Province, the Jangdo Island High Moor is found in the summit of an island mountain. Water from rain, snow, fog, and frost collects in the bowl-shaped summit, which has a surface entirely lined with solid granite. The soil found here is rich in organic content and highly absorbent, allowing it to filter impurities from the water, which eventually makes its way into underground streams and mountain streams that flow down the slopes to the villages below—by which time it is pure enough for use as drinking water. The locals have first-hand knowledge of the importance of wetlands as water purification agents. Today, the Jangdo Island High Moor is being studied for its natural ability to supply clean water. It is also known for its ecological diversity—at once a paradise for various predatory birds, local plants (including the wind orchid, a Class 1 endangered species), and even tropical birds like the light-vented bulbul.

The Suncheon Bay Protected Area

The Suncheon Bay Protected Area and the Boseong Beolgyo Tidal Flats Protected Area are grouped together into the Ramsar-registered Suncheon Bay region. The landscape of this bay is notably diverse, with tracts of reed thickets interspersed with red *Suaeda japonicus*, forming patterns like an engraved seal. In the winter, migratory birds like the hooded crane take flight over the reed fields of the ocean basin that penetrates deep into the land. For this reason, Suncheon Bay has become known as the "reed paradise" and "home of the hooded crane." Some 220 other species of birds have been sighted here, of which 35 are endangered, including the hooded crane, black-faced spoonbill, Oriental stork, peregrine falcon, and common buzzard.

The vibrant scenery of Suncheon Bay can be attributed to a harmonious melding of natural influences. In particular, the streams of Dongcheon and Isacheon steadily empty their waters into the bay, providing a constant source of fresh water for the tidal flats and diluting the sea water's salt content, thus allowing freshwater reeds and the saltwater *Suaeda japonicus* to coexist there. These brackish conditions have enabled the area to become an estuary salt marsh. Most of the estuaries in Korea are blocked off by dams or irrigation reservoirs for agricultural purposes, so Suncheon Bay is indeed a rarity, making it all the more meaningful and valuable.

The Boseong Beolgyo Tidal Flats

Across the bay, the Boseong Beolgyo Tidal Flats are particularly well known for their rich variety of sea life. This is Korea's primary stomping ground for the Malaysian cockle and mudskipper, which net tidy profits for local fishermen. Shellfish such as the jackknife clam and Asian clam also add to the economic value of these flats.

Ganghwa Maehwamareum Habitat

Rice paddies function as manmade wetlands, as they can be unique ecosystems unto themselves, and they are now considered eligible for registration as Ramsar sites. Korea's Ganghwa Maehwamareum Habitat became the world's first rice paddy to earn formal designation as a Ramsar site at the 10th Ramsar Conference, when the rice paddies in Asia's monsoonal regions were recognized for their ability to support biodiversity.

Fishermen at the Boseong Beolgyo Tidal Flat

Maehwamareum habitat in Ganghwa-do

Korea is now shedding new light on rice paddies as habitats for endangered species and adopting measures for their preservation. This has led to research on the plants and animals that populate the paddies and on the identification of representative species. For instance, the Maehwamareum (Korean water crowfoot) was long thought to be extinct until growths were discovered in the rice paddies of Ganghwa-do Island. As the land areas were slated for redistribution and eventual development, the National Trust intervened and acquired the site. Though it covers a relatively small area, the paddy was registered as a Ramsar site to assure its continued protection. Nearby areas have adopted organic farming practices in an effort to promote the Maehwamareum's survival, and the locally grown rice is marketed as "Maehwamareum rice," which adds to the revenues of the area's farmers. The area has also become very popular as an ecological and historical attraction for visitors, with a trail for observing the Maehwamareum, an education center, the nearby tidal flats, and assorted historic sites.

When farmed organically, the paddies can provide a home to over 100 species of aquatic plants and a variety of waterborne creatures, such as the horseshoe crab, rice paddy snail, water snail, crucian carp, and mudfish. The Maehwamareum is in full bloom in early May, just before the farmers transplant the rice seedlings.

UPO WETLANDS: A MASTERPIECE OF NATURE

The largest and oldest wetlands in Korea, the Upo Wetlands are also the most popular, with over 1 million tourists visiting the site annually. Located in Changnyeong-gun, Gyeongsangnam-do Province, they are (like other inland wetland areas) considerably shallower than a lake, with depths reaching no more than one meter. The *Joseonji (Geographical Records of Joseon)* contains a passage reading, "The heavens have Cheonji Lake atop Mt. Baekdusan, while the earth has the Upo Wetlands in Changnyeong." While ancient Koreans regarded Cheonji Lake as sacred ground, they also revered Upo Wetlands and showed great respect for its intriguing environment.

Mt. Uhangsan juts majestically from the site. Its name, meaning "cow neck," comes from its resemblance to a cow bending its head to drink the marsh water. For years, cows were brought to graze along the water's edge, which led to the area earning the name, "Cow Flats." During their colonial rule of Korea in the early 20th century, Japanese authorities changed place names from Korean Hangeul to Chinese characters, and as a result the Cow Flats (Sobeol) became "Upo."

It is believed that the Upo Wetlands were created at a time when Cretaceous dinosaurs roamed the land. Following the Ice Age, the topography along the Nakdonggang River underwent a radical transformation. As glaciers melted and the river overflowed, silt and sand deposits blocked the entrance to today's Topyeong Stream, causing the waters to accumulate and form a vast lake. Over time, this lake turned into the Upo Wetlands. The wetlands consist of four marsh areas: Upo, Mokpo, Sajipo, and Jjokjibeol. Mokpo ("tree flats") is so named because it is where trees ended up after being felled by heavy rains. Sajipo ("sand flats") takes its name from its expansive sand tracts, while Jjokjibeol ("scrap flats") earned its name for its smaller scale.

As Korea's industrialization steadily gained momentum in the 1970s, the government began reclaiming wetland areas in an effort to increase available agricultural land. Based on accounts from scholars and local residents, the original Upo Wetlands covered an estimated 11 km^2—roughly five times larger than its current area. Its freshwater capacity is thought to have been 1.25 billion tons, which is about equivalent to the reservoir at Andong Dam in Gyeongsangbuk-do Province. The area was designated by the Ministry of Environment as an ecological and scenic preserve encompassing about 8.54 km^2 of land, with a water surface area of 2.3 km^2.

As the Seasons Change in Upo . . .

In spring, the weeping willow and purple willow come to life. Harbingers of spring include the adonis, Japanese witch hazel, and Japanese cornel dogwood. Chinese milk vetch also boasts a vibrant appearance. The aquatic plant that attracts the most attention, though, is the prickly water lily, with its large leaves that can reach about two meters in diameter. Although they are protected as an endangered species, one can see thousands of them in the water in midsummer. Water shield plants are another important aspect of the native aquatic plant life. They were once such a popular food source that locals would say, "The three best foods are mountain ginseng, wild grass ginseng, and water shield plants." Around this time, magpies and other sedentary birds get busy building nests ahead of the summer breeding season.

In summer, barefoot women venture into the marshy waters to harvest snails, making the human presence an integral part of the wetlands ecosystem. The long-tail tadpole shrimp (named an endangered species) can be found merrily swimming in the water. Its back is covered with an armored shell composed of 30 to 40 segments, while in the middle of the back, toward the front, sits a pair of large eyes. Resident mammals include the small-eared cat, which sits at the top of the food chain and can be seen stalking the local birds. The predator vs. prey scenes here are similar to those you might find in the Okavango Delta or Serengeti. An endangered species of otters also makes its home in the marshy waters. Prior to Korea's industrialization, otters numbered in the hundreds, but they have recently experienced such a drastic decline that it is difficult to spot even one.

In autumn, one can readily sense the area's primeval nature while watching the early morning mist rise from the marsh waters—a scene like a traditional landscape painting. On rainy days, melancholy steals over the heart. The green carpet changes in the bright autumn sunlight, which gives way to a chorus of insects as fireflies stage a delicate festival of light. From the water, tiny water fringes lift their heads to take in the view. All manner of insects—water striders, water scorpions, diving beetles—can be seen scurrying about.

In winter, the wetlands serve as a perfect stopover for migratory birds. As plants succumb to autumn's coolness and wind, they make room for these birds. Poetic sentiments are aroused in the heart of anyone fortunate enough to see flocks of speckled teal taking flight against the sunset, or to simply watch the mallard, bean goose, whooper swan, spoonbill, or mandarin duck search for food or take a moment to relax.

THE FUTURE OF THE WETLANDS

With some 70% of Korea's terrain is covered by mountains, its inland wetlands are rather small in scale. The ones along the west coast, however, are among the largest in the world. Unfortunately, Korea, like other East Asian countries, has pushed large-scale land reclamation projects with little consideration for the need to protect its tidal flats. In the future, much will need to be done to rehabilitate wetlands that have already been lost to development, while protecting those that are threatened. Korea has long been behind the times with its conservation measures, wise use of the coastal wetlands ecosystem, and protection of the natural habitats of migratory birds and waterfowl.

Fortunately, public awareness of the importance of wetlands protection has grown since the late 1990s. After the Ramsar Conference, Korea's Ministry of Environment increased the number of Ramsar sites in Korea to 18, and made plans to increase the number of protected wetland areas to 30, by 2012, while taking steps for the conservation of at least 20% of Korea's coastal wetlands by 2017. It also intends to restore 81 km^2 (about 10%) of currently reclaimed wetlands by 2017. The government is investing 200 billion won (about $180 million) into transforming the Upo Wetlands into a premier ecotourism attraction.

Ecology specialists have called for development to focus on cultural content, rather than just physical improvements like new roads and buildings. (The potential of this content can be witnessed in the 600,000 visitors who flock annually to Walden Pond in Massachusetts to enjoy the tranquil nature that so inspired Henry David Thoreau.) They also recommend efforts to preserve the natural ecosystem by relocating buildings from nearby areas so as to curtail environmental pollution, while encouraging organic farming in the areas around the wetlands.

Above all else, development should not do any damage to the wetlands' primeval nature. Any restoration of the Nakdonggang River should be carried out after first considering its potential impact on the ecological treasure trove of the Upo Wetlands. As much as riverbed dredging helps to promote flood control abilities and protect the natural ecosystem, it is essential that the proper water levels in the Upo Wetlands and other sites be maintained in order to sustain the primeval splendor that has endured the passage of 140 million years. There are valuable lessons to be learned from ecotourism sites like Walden Pond, the Mai Po Marshes in Hong Kong, the Kushiro Wetlands in Japan, and the Boondall Wetlands in Australia.

FROM RECLAMATION TO CONSERVATION

There are certain positive signs of Korea taking the first steps in shifting its focus from reclamation to conservation. One example is the reclamation project planned for Seocheon-gun County in Chungcheongnam-do Province: the original proposal has since been replaced with a more environment-friendly alternative. The government also issued the Seocheon Declaration, announcing its intentions of canceling the grand reclamation project in the area and transforming Seocheon into a center for visiting and studying the tidal flats. This is being taken as a signal of the adoption of sustainable use patterns for Korean tidal flats. Another fortunate development is the establishment of visitor facilities at Suncheon Bay, offering a successful model of ecotourism.

The Suncheon Bay wetlands provide a lesson in balancing wetlands conservation with ecotourism needs. In addition to its intertidal salt marsh areas and reed tracts, Suncheon Bay now offers much to see and enjoy with the development of the site as an ecotourism destination, including an ecology hall, astronomical observatory, migratory bird-watching activities, and a Tidal Flats Observatory. A variety of other steps are being taken to promote sustainability, including the use of tour buses and bicycles as a way of curtailing the volume of vehicle traffic around the bay. This shows that conservation and prudence, when properly implemented, can complement each other.

MIGRATORY BIRDS

As a Far Eastern country, Korea serves as an ideal stopover for migratory birds, a place where they can find food and prepare for the remainder of their journey. The west coast is home to expansive tidal flats, which offer food to the snipes, plovers, and the like. The islands scattered off the west coast are also important stopovers. And Korea's demilitarized zone (DMZ), long a no-man's-land, has become a paradise for rare migratory birds as well. This barrier, which so painfully separates the two Koreas, poses no such obstacle for the migratory birds that freely traverse the manmade boundary.

Of the birds that flock to Korea, the Eurasian spoonbill is a relatively rare winter visitor that can be observed in Korea's wetlands. Measuring about 86 cm in length, it settles at coastal areas, riverbanks, and rice paddies, and primarily feeds on fish, frogs, and beetles. There are fewer than 100,000 remaining in the world.

Birds flock to Junam Wetland Park in Changwon

1. The Chinese egret is protected as a natural monument, with only about 1,800 to 2,500 known to exist worldwide, making it a "vulnerable" species.

2. The black-faced spoonbill swishes its characteristic broad bill sideways to catch freshwater fish, frogs, and tadpoles. It is extremely cautious and thus difficult to approach. With a worldwide population estimated at less than 700, it has been declared an "endangered" species.

3. The hooded crane appears in small numbers in Korea. In spring and autumn, flocks that wintered in Japan stop in Korea in numbers that reach up to 4,000. It stands about one meter tall, with a wingspan of 48 to 53 cm.

4. The red-crowned crane prefers wetlands with thick reed growths. Flocks take flight in V-shaped patterns and appear in Korea in early November. Only about 1,690 to 2,040 are known to remain worldwide. In Korea, they are protected as a natural monument.

Chapter Five

TREASURE OF NATURE, JEJU

I t is not hard to see why Jeju-do Island is so loved by the people of Korea, and virtually everyone else who visits. It is positively covered in fantastic natural features, which have led many travelers to describe it variously as "Asia's Mediterranean coast," the "jewel of Korea," and even "paradise on earth." UNESCO seemed to agree, designating Jeju Volcanic Island and Lava Tubes as a World Heritage Site, and recognizing the entire island as a Global Geopark in 2007. Earlier, in 2002, it named the island a Biosphere Reserve. In these ways and more, the island's natural beauty has been the subject of both global praise and calls for safeguarding. J.M.G Le Clezio, the Nobel Laureate in Literature, described Jeju as following, "At the door between the infiniteness of the Pacific Ocean and the vastness of the most expensive and populous continent on the planet." Living in the midst of such beauty, the islanders are unsurprisingly friendly and warm, and have developed a culture that is distinct from the one found on the mainland across the Korea Strait.

OLLE TRAILS

It has been said that Jeju-do Island is rich in three things—wind, rocks, and women—while lacking in three others—beggars, thieves, and locked gates. "Locked gates" is the operative phrase here, as it seems the island's roads are indeed open to any and all who decide to visit. This is particularly evident in the famous Olle trails (Olle-gil), which will soon fully encircle the length of the 175-kilometer-long island. Currently, 20 courses are open to the public, with more planned for completion soon.

The word *olle* comes from the local dialect and describes a narrow path leading from the front door of one's house to the street outside. In a sense, the Olle trails were so named to invite travelers to the island: through them, Jeju-do is essentially throwing its front door open and welcoming the world to its doorstep. *Olle* also happens to translate into the phrase "Won't you come?" in

Seongsan Ilchulbong

Seongsanpo,
Olle trail Route 1

standard Korean—Jeju Olle can thus be translated as "Won't you come to Jeju-do?" These sweetly named trails were the brainchild of a former magazine editor, Seo Myung-sook who upon walking the length of the famed Camino de Santiago road (a 800-kilometer trek from France to Spain), decided to create a similar trail in Korea, and particularly on her home island. With the help of a survey team, she explored the island and found undiscovered roads and hidden pathways that might appeal to fellow trekkers. Today, the Jeju-do Olle trails are so popular that *olle* has become a generic byword for any forest trails or pathways, even those that are not actually on Jeju-do Island. (For example, one popular public trail leading up Mt. Bukhansan in Seoul is called the "Bukhansan Dulle.") The Jeju-do Olle trails, however, set themselves apart from other roads—such as the Santiago road and Japan's Shikoku Pilgrimage Road—with a unique scenic beauty that only their home island can offer.

By taking a different trail, visitors can experience something new every time. For example, Route 1, which was opened in September 2007 as the first Olle course, passes along several *oreums*—the crests of small inactive volcanoes. These *oreums* are part of what make the island's scenery unique. In addition to actual volcanoes, the island also boasts jagged, soot-black volcanic rocks scattered all along its coast. All these and more can be viewed from Route 1, along with Seongsan Ilchulbong ("sunrise peak"), which is included as part of Jeju-do's World Heritage Site. Some courses, like Route 5, stay very close to the coast, offering trekkers the chance to dip their tired feet in the seawater or stop at local villages to grab a bite before heading on to the next trail. These seaside trails are fairly leisurely compared to courses like Route 6, which demands the visitor's full concentration seeing as it meanders past cultural and ecological sites like Cheonjiyeon Waterfall and Eodolgae Rock. Route 8 coasts along the shore before reaching a formation of stone pillars.

With all these rocks and stones on the island, it should come as no surprise that one of the island's symbols is made of stone: the *dol harubang*, large mushroom-shaped basalt rock structures that are placed throughout the island for good luck, protection, and fertility. Visitors to the Olle trails will chance upon these structures quite often during their trip. Another ubiquitous sight is pampas, a tall grass with bluish-green or silvery grey leaves that make for a gorgeous sight when they sway in the wind. Depending on the route, visitors may also stumble upon Buddhist temples

Dol harubang, or "Grandfather Rock"

tucked deep in the mountains or come across salt fields where farmers can be seen toiling away, gathering sun-baked salt.

The island is 130 km south of the mainland, making for a warmer climate that turns walking along the trails into even more of a pleasurable experience. Routes are easy to find: clearly visible blue arrows nudge the traveler in the right direction. These arrows are typically found scrawled on stone walls in villages and on rocks by the shore. When none are present, visitors can look for yellow or blue ribbons tied around tree branches. People who come here are also advised to take the necessary precautions before launching on their treks—wear comfortable shoes, bring a raincoat or windbreaker (the weather can be unpredictable), drink plenty of fluids, and get sufficient rest in between walks. Most importantly, visitors are asked to travel responsibly and sustainably, abiding by the spirit of the Olle trails and the mantra *nolmeong, shimeong, georumeong*—"play, rest, walk."

THE VOLCANIC ISLAND

As touched upon in the above section, Jeju-do is rich in *oreums*, also known as lava tubes. These are scattered throughout the island—indeed, the entire island is volcanic, created by eruptions 2 million years ago, which is why it is so generously endowed with basalt rocks. Its shores are dotted with these rocks, too, giving it quite a different landscape from the typical white-sands vibe found at most other beaches. These soot-black rocks can make for a majestic sight, especially when frothy, blustering waves are crashing down over them. As for the *oreums*, there are roughly 370 of them all over the island, along with over 160 underground lava caves. It is rare for so many volcanoes and caves to be gathered on one small island—no doubt one of the key reasons Jeju Volcanic Island and Lava Tubes was designated a World Heritage Site. These small volcanoes, or lava tubes, connect back to what is arguably the island's main feature: Mt. Hallasan. The 370-odd tubes are empty now, but back in the Cretaceous days magma flowed through them freely. Today, they are popular tourist attractions, as evidenced by the many Olle trails that connect to them. One of the caves, the Manjanggul Lava Tube, houses the world's largest known lava column. While the cave itself is seven kilometers long, only a section

Lava column, Manjanggul Cave

of it is accessible to the public. The tube is part of the Geomunoreum Lava Tube System, the largest network of lava tubes on the island. Four others can also be found here; these were only recently opened to the public and are still relatively untouched.

The tallest mountain in South Korea, standing proud at 1,950 meters above sea level, is Mt. Hallasan, a dormant volcano with a lake situated at its peak. Ensconced in its own national park reserve, its location puts it at the very heart of the island. In addition to being very popular with visitors, it is also scientifically significant, as it is the only mountain in the country with plant distribution in three temperature zones (frigid, temperate, and subtropical), beginning at its low-lying base and extending up to its

Wild deer on the slopes
of Mt. Hallasan

higher altitudes. Over 1,500 plants and 17 mammals have been noted so far. The island split off from the mainland over 10,000 years ago, and several flora and fauna have been found dating from around that time, making them indigenous to the island. Some of these species are considered endangered, including the Siberian Roe Deer and Leopard Cat. The island also boasts many flowers, with its rape blossoms a sight of particular beauty—vast fields of them can be found all around, especially on the 43-kilometer road connecting the island's two major urban areas, Jeju City and Seogwipo. The broad stretches of rape blossoms are popular with tourists, and honeymooners in particular. Another popular attraction is Seongsan Ilchubong, yet another volcano, which juts up 180 meters above sea level. The peak takes its name from its spectacular view of the sunrise, which makes it a favorite destination among Koreans in general—mainlanders included—who come on December 31 in the hopes of catching a glimpse of the first rays of the New Year sun. Unfortunately, the area can be foggy on most days, but the payoff is well worth the gamble.

Korea's largest island is also flanked by many smaller islands that are as beautiful as their sister, if not more so. Udo Island is the largest of these smaller satellites, and second only to Mt. Hallasan in its popularity with tourists. Its beaches are quite beautiful with their white sands (Hagosudong Beach) and coral (Sanhosa Beach). Mara-do Island, another satellite, is Korea's southernmost island. It is rather small—it takes only an hour and a half to cover its entire area. Visitors can take a ferry from a pier on the main island and go sightseeing in the sea caves, or trek up the smaller island's steep cliffs and black rock formations.

For visitors who've already hit the beach and the Olle trails and would prefer a nice, quiet walk in the shade, Jeju-do also offers many forest pathways, both natural and manmade. Located near the base of Mt. Hallasan, Jeolmul Recreational Forest is thick and dense—Japanese cedar and black pine trees planted here in the early 1970s have since grown to incredible sizes. Both types were planted

Seobin Baeksa Beach, Udo Island

for their hardiness, a necessity due to the island's strong sea winds. Jeolmul (literally "temple water") Forest has a hiking path that stretches around the woods, along with a place where visitors can learn how to grow shiitake mushrooms. Another forest, Bijarim, is located farther away on the outer rim of the island. It's known for its distinguished-looking nutmeg trees, which number over 2,500. Some are said to be over 800 years old, making this one of the world's few natural nutmeg forests. Indeed, the new millennium nutmeg—the oldest variety in Korea—can be found here.

LIFESTYLES AND PEOPLE

Along with its aforementioned three "plenties" (wind, rocks, and women), the island is also known for its *sambo*, literally the "three boasts"—its language, its underwater resources, and its ecological treasures. These help to define Jeju-do's culture as distinct from that of the mainland. Its variant of Korean is unique, as evidenced by words like *olle* that are still in wide use to this day. (Mainlanders often have trouble understanding the indigenous dialect.) And, of course, the island's nature is also noteworthy, with many species endemic to the area. By virtue of being an island, Jeju-do has underwater resources that are both plentiful and magnificent; its clear waters teem with species of coral and fish.

Food of Jeju

The island's seafood is also famed for its freshness and variety. *Okdom* (sea bream) is called the "king of all fish" and served by locals to special guests. It may be served grilled, roasted, fried, or cooked in stew or porridge. Porridge is another popular dish—virtually any seafood can be chopped, tossed into a pot with some rice, and simmered to perfection for a hearty, satisfying bowl.

Abalone porridge, or *jeonbokjuk*, is perhaps the best known and most nutritious. Along with seafood, the island is known for its famed *heukdwaeji* (literally "black pig"). The bellies from these pigs (called *samgyeopsal*) are especially tasty, with a richer texture than the traditional variety. (Some of the more famous black pork restaurants on Jeju-do Island have opened chains on the mainland as well.) Additionally, the island has a long history of horse breeding, which has spawned a culinary tradition of eating horsemeat—a tradition that is only found here.

Another famed feature of the island are its vast stretches of fruit orchards, almost all of which grow the popular *gamgyul* (sweet tangerines) or Jeju-do's own *hallabong*, a hybrid citrus fruit. The warmer climate here makes the island an optimal location for growing citrus fruits; indeed, it would be no exaggeration to say that

1. *Gamgyul* 2. *Heukdwaeji* 3. *Okdom* 4. *Jeonbokjuk*

almost all the islands grow and sell these tangerines as a sideline. The *gamgyul* were traditionally considered such a delicacy that they were served to royals during the Joseon Dynasty. Named for Mt. Hallasan, the *hallabong* is known for its particularly sweet flavor and slightly higher price tag. Its name comes from its bulb-like shape that narrows at the top, making it resemble the cone of a mountain.

Jeju Haenyeo

Some of the prominent characteristics of the villages here are their traditional rites, women divers, and stouthearted fishermen. Residents have experienced pleasure and sorrow for generation upon generation in their pursuit of coexistence with the indomitable and tumultuous sea.

Korea's women divers, or *haenyeo* (literally "sea women"), are no doubt the most colorful of Korea's seaside residents. Diving repeatedly into the ocean's perilous depths to support their family, they are a perfect example of the hardiness of Korean women. Jeju's *haenyeo* are particularly well known for their extraordinary ability to remain out at sea for five hours or longer. Pushing the limits of physical endurance, they continue diving even when they are so nauseous from the turbulent currents that motion-sickness medicine provides no relief. Unlike tangerines or other land-based crops, the ocean's bounty can be gathered and sold for cash on a daily basis. The lung capacity of a *haenyeo* has a direct bearing on her income: the longer she can remain underwater, the more she can earn. It takes 10 to 15 seconds to reach the sea floor, more than 30 seconds to locate the targeted abalone and top shell, and 20 seconds to pry them off the rocks and secure them in mesh bags. A diver's time underwater is limited to about one minute or so; staying underwater for too long can lead to respiratory complications and even drowning.

With their extraordinary lung capacity and aversion to risk, the women divers here are enigmas, figures widely known in Korea and abroad. Their remarkable abilities enable them to dive to depths of 20 meters and remain underwater for about two minutes without the aid of any breathing apparatus. Foreign medical researchers have taken note; indeed, in the 1960s the US State Department conducted studies on the women divers of Korea and Japan as part of an effort to bolster the efficiency of its underwater projects and the capabilities of its naval personnel. The *haenyeo* of Jeju-do are known to dive 15 or so days a month. The frequency varies according to ocean and seasonal conditions, but from a physiological perspective it is truly astonishing that they can dive practically every other day. They can be seen gathering abalone just before giving birth, and returning to the blue seas just three or four days afterward. This work ethic stems not just from physical capability but from a tenacious mindset that enables them to accept the perils of the sea every time they plunge into its waters.

While the *haenyeo* and other residents of the island are known for their resourcefulness and hardiness, they are also incredibly generous. Indeed, this generosity of spirit is one of the three "beauties" of this southern isle, together with its nature and its fruit harvests. Of all that the island has to offer, this is perhaps its greatest attraction—its smiling inhabitants warmly beckoning all visitors to their home island. *Jeju olle?*

SAMSEONGHYEOL

Jeju-do Island is rich in myths and legends. Perhaps one of the more interesting is the one about the birth of Tamna, the ancient kingdom that ruled the island until it was absorbed by the mainland's Joseon Dynasty in 1404. According to legend, three demigods with the last names Ko, Yang, and Bu sprung up from three holes in the ground. Records such as *Yeongjuji* and *Goryeosa Jiriji* describe them as having lived as hunter-gatherers until three princesses from the kingdom of Byeokrang came to them with cattle and the seeds of five grains. After marrying these women, the demigods formed a community that later became the Tamna Kingdom.

In interpretations of the legend, the three demigods are explained as three powerful figures in the island's history who were represented as gods to lend them more authority. The three "princesses" probably refer to outside forces who introduced the island to agriculture. As the formerly nomadic land came together with a pre-modern agricultural society, a new kingdom was born.

Visitors to the island can still see the holes in the ground where the legendary figures are said to have emerged. Shaped in a triangle with one hole on top of the other two, Samseonghyeol (literally "holes of three names") is located in the midst of a lush forest and has been designated National Historic Landmark No. 134. One of the three holes is said to be so deep that it flows into the sea, while another hole has succumbed to the pressures of time—only traces of it can be seen today. Even now, memorial rites are held every April 10 and October 10 by the royal descendants. Visitors can access the exhibition hall nearby, which also screens an animated version of the story of how the island kingdom came to be.

KOREA'S TRAILS

Korea has many mountain trails that allow visitors to tread over soft beds of leaves and scamper over big boulders, all while enjoying the fresh air and gorgeous scenery. Of these trails (*gil* in Korean), Jeju-do Island's Olle-gil system is perhaps the most famous, but there are many mainland trails as well. Mt. Jirisan, which stands 1,915 meters tall, overlooks the Jirisan Dulle-gil, a path that runs for a full 300 km around the mountain and along local villages and roads. Trekking along these trails grants visitors a glimpse into the lives of local inhabitants, who use the same roads to head to the markets or call on their friends. If you're in Gyeongsangbuk-do Province, consider a day's excursion to Yeongdeok Blue Road, officially designated by the government as a Culture & Ecology Trail in 2009. Located along the eastern coast of Korea, the trail goes on for 50 km from Gangguhang Port to Goraebul Beach. Trekkers can take in the sea views, coastal villages, and beaches,

while enjoying fresh seafood along the way. And Seoul, sprawling metropolis that it is, is also home to the Mt. Bukhansan Dulle-gil, totaling 70 km in length and linking the forest paths of Mt. Bukhansan and Mt. Dobongsan. Over 1,300 different species of plants and animals are found along the 21 sections of the trails: 12 sections along Mt. Bukhansan (opened in September 2010) and nine on Mt. Dobongsan (June 2011). Each is unique, and they are named accordingly: Sonamusup-gil ("pine tree forest trail"), Myeongsang-gil ("path of meditation"), and so forth. When visiting these *gil* sites, it's best to put on some athletic or hiking footwear, with an optional pair of sandals for the coastal areas. Layers and waterproof clothing are recommended, as the weather might be unpredictable on certain parts of the trails.

Yeongdeok Blue Road

INFORMATION

FURTHER INFORMATION

BOOKS ON KOREA'S NATURE & TOURISM

Robert Koehler, *Seoul Selection Guides: SEOUL*.
Seoul: Seoul Selection, 2009.

Roger Shepherd & Andrew Douch, *Baekdu Daegan Trail*.
Seoul: Seoul Selection, 2010.

Brenda Paik Sunoo, *Moon Tides: Jeju Island Grannies of the Sea*.
Seoul: Seoul Selection, 2011.

Anne Hilty, *Jeju Island: Reaching to the Core of Beauty*.
Seoul: Seoul Selection, 2011.

Robert Koehler, *Seoul Selection Guides: KOREA*.
Seoul: Seoul Selection, 2012.

Beverlee Barnet, *Camping in Korean National Parks*.
Seoul: Seoul Selection, 2012.

WEBSITES

Tourism

- Korea Tourism Organization — http://www.visitkorea.or.kr
- Hangang Park — http://www.hangang.seoul.go.kr
- Korea National Park Service — http://main.knps.or.kr
- Cittaslow Korea Network — http://www.cittaslow.kr
- Jeju Olle — http://www.jejuolle.org
- Templestay — http://www.templestay.com
- Exploring Korea — http://www.exploringkorea.com

Hiking Communities

- International Guides of Korea (IGK) — http://iguidekorea.com
- Hike Korea — http://www.hikekorea.com
- Facebook 'Seoul Hiking Group' Page — http://www.facebook.com/groups/seoulhiking

HANGANG FESTIVALS

April

- Hangang Yeouido Spring Flower Festival — http://tour.ydp.go.kr/SpFestival/main.html

May

- Green Plugged Seoul — http://www.greenplugged.com
- Rape Flower Festival at Hangang Seoraeseom

June

- Hangang Seoul Marathon — http://www.hangangseoul.co.kr

October

- Seoul International Fireworks Festival — http://www.hanwhapyro.com
- Hangang Literary Festivals in Seonyudo — http://www.hanganglf.org
- Koreacup Paper Airplane Competition — http://www.paperairplane.co.kr

KOREAN NATIONAL PARKS

Mountainous Parks

- **Seoraksan National Park**
  Address 43, Seorak-dong, Sokcho-si, Gangwon-do
  Tel +82-33-636-7700, 7702~3

- **Bukhansan National Park**
  Address San 1-1, Jeongneung-dong, Seongbuk-gu, Seoul
  Tel +82-2-909-0497~8, 918-9063

- **Odaesan National Park**
  Address 75-6, Ganpyeong-ri, Jinbu-myeon, Pyeongchang-gun, Gangwon-do
  Tel +82-33-332-6417, 6494

- **Chiaksan National Park**
  Address 900, Hakgok-ri, Socho-myeon, Wonju-si, Gangwon-do
  Tel +82-33-732-4634, 5231, 1445

- **Sobaeksan National Park**
  Address San 86-51, Sucheol-ri, Punggi-eup, Yeongju-si, Gyeongsangbuk-do
  Tel +82-54-638-6196

- **Woraksan National Park**
  Address 693-1, Songgye-ri, Hansu-myeon, Jecheon-si, Chungcheongbuk-do
  Tel +82-43-653-3250

- **Gyeryongsan National Park**
  Address 777, Hakbong-ri, Banpo-myeon, Gongju-si, Chungcheongnam-do
  Tel +82-42-825-3002~3, 9597

- **Songnisan National Park**
  Address 19-1, Sangpan-ri, Naesongni-myeon, Boeun-gun, Chungcheongbuk-do
  Tel +82-43-542-5267~9

- **Juwangsan National Park**
  Address 406, Sangui-ri, Budong-myeon, Cheongsong-gun, Gyeongsangbuk-do
  Tel +82-54-873-0014~5

- **Deogyusan National Park**
  Address 411-8, Samgong-ri, Seolcheon-myeon, Muju-gun, Jeollabuk-do
  Tel +82-63-322-3174~5

- **Gayasan National Park**
  Address 123-1, Guwon-ri, Gaya-myeon, Hapcheon-gun, Gyeongsangnam-do
  Tel +82-55-932-7810, 7830, 7850

- **Naejangsan National Park**
  Address 59-10, Naejang-dong, Jeongeup-si, Jeollabuk-do
  Tel +82-63-538-7875~7

- **Jirisan National Park**
  Address 7 Deoksandaepo-ro, Sicheon-myeon, Sancheong-gun, Gyeongsangnam-do
  Tel +82-55-972-7771~2

- **Wolchulsan National Park**
  Address 484-50, Gaesin-ri, Yeongam-eup, Yeongam-gun, Jeollanam-do
  Tel +82-61-473-5210~1, 5112

- **Hallasan National Park**
  Address San 220-1, Haean-dong, Jeju-si, Jeju Special Self Governing Province
  Tel +82-64-713-9950

Marine & Coastal Parks

- **Taeanhaean National Park**
  Address 9 Gwisil-gil, Jangsan-ri, Taean-eup, Taean-gun, Chungcheongnam-do
  Tel +82-41-672-9737~8, 7267

- **Byeonsanbando National Park**
  Address 415-24, Daehang-ri, Byeonsan-myeon, Buan-gun, Jeollabuk-do
  Tel +82-63-582-7808

- **Hallyeohaesang National Park**
  Address 634, Sangju-ri, Sangju-myeon, Namhae-gun, Gyeongsangnam-do
  Tel +82-55-863-3521~2

- **Dadohaehaesang National Park**
  Address 1240-8, Gaepo-ri, Wando-eup, Wando-gun, Jeollanam-do
  Tel +82-61-554-5474

Historical Park

- **Gyeongju National Park**
  Address 958-6, Yonggang-dong, Gyeongju-si, Gyeongsangbuk-do
  Tel +82-54-741-7612~4

The content of this book has been compiled, edited, and supplemented by Amber Hyun Jung Kim from the following articles published in:

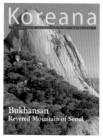

KOREANA, Vol.18, No.1 Spring 2004

"The Feng Shui (Pungsu) of Mt. Bukhansan"
 by Zho In-choul
"Bukhansan Keeps Alive Shaman Traditions"
 by Kim Duk-muk
"Bukhansanseong Fortress" by Nah Kag-soon
"Mt. Bukhansan's Charm and Inspiration"
 by Um Hong-gil, Kwak Won-joo, Lee Sung-boo
"People Who Climb Mt. Bukhansan" by Kim Woo-sun

KOREANA, Vol. 18, No.2, Summer 2004

"Historic River Flowing Through the Korean Peninsula"
 by Shin Jung-il
"Driving Force behind Korea's Economic Development"
 by Song Do-young
"Preservation of the Hangang's Ecology" by Kim Jae-il
"Center of Urban Life and Diversion from the Mundane"
 by Choi Tae-won

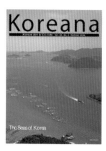

KOREANA, Vol.20, No.2 Summer 2006

"The Ocean's Influence on the Korean People"
 by Na Gyung-soo
"Korea Sphere of Maritime Influence"
 by Youn Myung-chul
"Korean Waters Abound with Marine Life"
 by Kim Woong-seo
"Mining the Ocean Depths for Energy Resources"
 by Kim Hyun-tae
"The Vibrant Sea and Its Coastal Residents"
 by Nam Sung-suk

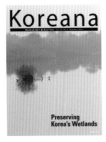

PHOTOGRAPHS

Korea Tourism Organization Cover, 5, 7, 8, 21 (top), 22, 23, 24, 31, 32, 35, 36, 37, 38, 40, 41, 42 (top), 46, 47, 49, 51, 52, 53, 55, 56, 58, 59, 61, 63, 67, 68, 70, 72, 75, 77, 78, 81, 82, 83, 87, 89, 92, 93
Jeju Special Self-Governing Province 85, 86
Yeongdeok-gun 94
Gansong Art Museum 13
Yonhap Photo 14, 34, 36, 41, 45, 65, 69, 74, 79
Image Today 36, 42 (bottom), 47, 79
Robert Koehler 15, 21 (bottom), 28, 32, 59 (top), 89
Ryu Seung-hoo 11, 16, 18, 26, 27, 50, 54, 95
Brenda Paik Sunoo 90

CREDITS

Publisher	Kim Hyung-geun
Writer	Amber Hyun Jung Kim
Editor	Park Hye-young
Copy Editors	Colin A. Mouat, Daisy Larios
Designer	Shin Eun-ji